INCREASE GOD'S WAY

ISBN-13: 978-0-9702911-7-2
ISBN-10: 0-9702911-7-5
Unless otherwise stated, all Scripture
quotations are taken from
The King James Version of the Bible.

Jerry Savelle Ministries International
P.O. Box 748
Crowley, TX 76036
(817) 297-3155
www.jerrysavelle.org

INCREASE
GOD'S WAY

Jerry Savelle

TABLE OF CONTENTS

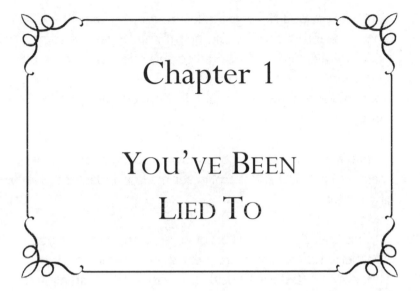

Chapter 1

You've Been Lied To

I was fed up! I had had enough! My wife, Carolyn, was always trying to get me to go to church. Dragging me to hear boring preachers. I hated it!

And here we go again. She's begging me to go with her. I told her I didn't care how much she begged. I was not going!

But this time, she told me that if I would go with her and if I didn't like this preacher, then she would NEVER ask me to go again.

Never? You promise you will never ask me to go again?" I asked.

"I'll never ask you to go again," said Carolyn.

That sounded like a good deal to me. If I went this one time, it meant that she would quit trying to get me to go. I made up my mind that I would go this one last time, sit on the back row, not believe a word that was said, and then she would never ask me to go again. It sounded like a good idea and that was my plan.

However, that's not quite how it worked out. I had been set up. God and Carolyn set me up. I was not planning on that.

This preacher was different. He wasn't like any other preacher I had every heard before. He reminded me of John Wayne. Before I knew it, I was actually listening to what he was saying. He got my attention. He spoke with authority like I had never heard. I will never forget the last words he said that night. He said, "If you believe it, it will work. If you don't, it won't. Goodnight." Then he walked off. That was it. He just walked off.

That night I went for one purpose – to never be asked to go again. Instead, my life was changed. I heard the gospel like I had never heard it before. It penetrated my hardness of heart. It penetrated all the unbelief in my mind. All of the excuses I had for running from God were all shattered that night. That night changed my life, and it has never been the same since. The man was Kenneth Copeland.

The next morning a lady from the church came by our house and said, "Jerry, I recorded all of the messages from

Kenneth Copeland, and the Lord told me to give them to you." And then she handed me a bag full of reel-to-reel tapes.

I said, "What am I supposed to do with these? I don't have any way to listen to them."

"You don't?" She asked.

"No."

"I'll be back." She ran off.

A few hours later she returned with the machine to play the tapes.

I set that big old machine (if you remember reel-to-reel tapes, you know what I am talking about) up in our spare bedroom and began to listen to them. All fourteen messages. I couldn't get enough. I was consumed with the Word that was preached. Once again, it was unlike any sermons I had ever heard. He kicked over every sacred cow, every religious tradition that I had ever heard. I couldn't believe it. I had never seen or heard anything like it, and surely not in the churches that I had attended.

I listened to those tapes over and over again. I got my Bible, my notebook, and my pen and I began to study the Word for myself. I studied it until his revelations became my revelations.

For the first time in my life I was studying the Bible. And do you know what I found out? I had been lied to. That's right, I was lied to. Good, well-meaning, sincere Christians had lied to me. They were very sincere, but they were sincerely wrong. They told me that God made people sick to teach them lessons. They told me things like, "That's right, you'd better fear God, boy, or He'll get ya." They said God loved poverty. They said God and poverty were linked together with a very short rope.

But, once I started reading and studying the Word for myself, I couldn't find any of that in the Bible. Instead, I found out that Jesus' stripes provided for my healing. I didn't have to be sick. Jesus had already paid the price for my health. I found out that I had been redeemed from the curse. And that God considered poverty a curse. I found out that I had a covenant with the Creator of the heavens and earth. And that covenant said that health, increase, and success belonged to me.

Now, you have to understand. I was in business for myself. I owned Jerry's Paint and Body Shop. And I was broke. I was in debt. My marriage less than perfect. And I got sick just like everyone else. As a matter of fact, we had a medicine cabinet in our bathroom full of medicine because that's the only way that we knew.

I thought that was just how it was supposed to be. I didn't know any better. I had never read the Bible before. I read hot rod magazines. I read car magazines. Not the

Bible. But when I did start reading it, my life and my perspective about life totally changed. Once again, I found out that God wanted to bless me. Little ol' me, average Jerry. That's right. He wanted me healthy, blessed, and prosperous. And I want to tell you right now, you've most likely been lied to just like I was. God wants you blessed! Yes, you.

GOD'S INTENT

God's original intent for mankind was that they should live a blessed life.

And God said, Let us make man in our image, after our likeness: and let them have dominion over the fish of the sea, and over the fowl of the air, and over the cattle, and over all the earth, and over every creeping thing that creepeth upon the earth.

So God created man in his own image, in the image of God created he him, male and female created he them.

And God blessed them, and God said unto them, Be fruitful, and multiply...

Genesis 1:26-28

What was the first thing God did after He created them? He blessed them. Genesis is the book of beginnings, and what I want you to see is that from the very beginning God intended man to live a blessed lifestyle.

Blessed literally means *empowered to prosper, to be empowered to prosper as a result of having God's favor bestowed on your life.* So immediately after creating man God empowered them to prosper. He caused His favor to be upon them. And then He told them to be fruitful and multiply. Most of the time, when we read that we think only about replenishing the earth through offspring. But to be fruitful also means to be successful in every endeavor. So God blessed them and then told them to be fruitful in every endeavor.

Now we know the story of how Adam blew it. Adam committed high treason in the garden of Eden, but even though Adam blew it, God's plan for mankind did not change. What happened? God literally started over with Noah and his family.

And God blessed Noah and his sons, and said unto them, Be fruitful, and multiply, and replenish the earth.

Genesis 9:1

Notice that even though Adam messed up, God's plan remained the same. The same thing that God told Adam and Eve in the garden is what He told Noah. His plan for mankind had not changed. He still wanted them blessed. He still wanted them to prosper and to be fruitful.

And God spake unto Noah, and to his sons with him, saying,

And I, behold, I establish my covenant with you, and with your seed after you.

Genesis 9:8,9

Notice that God not only establishes His covenant with Noah and his sons, but he wanted this to perpetuate from generation to generation.

God believes that if you can get a spiritual principle to work in at least three generations, then more than likely, it will continue through mankind. If you can get a man, his son, and his grandson all living the same principle, then it's likely that it will continue throughout that family.

And I can tell you that it works. I got it. I taught it to my children. They got it. And now they are teaching it to their children. And praise God, as long as there are Savelles on this planet, we are going to increase, we're going to prosper, we're going to be highly favored, and we're going to be blessed of God. And that's the way God wants it to be in your life and in your family's life as well.

One more example, in Genesis 12, God appears to a man by the name of Abram. And He says in Genesis 12:2 – *And I will make of thee a great nation, and I will bless thee, and make thy name great; and thou shalt be a blessing.*

Once again, God is perpetuating His original plan for mankind. Adam, Noah, Abraham, Isaac, Jacob. What is God doing? He is endeavoring to promote increase in the earth for His people.

What was Abraham's testimony? God said He was going to bless him and make his name great. And that's exactly what happened.

Now Abraham was old, well advanced in years, and the Lord had blessed Abraham in all things.

Genesis 24:1 (Amplified Bible)

So here's Abraham. When he was well stricken in age, his testimony was that God had empowered him to prosper. God had highly favored him. God had brought increase into every area of his life.

GOD'S INTENT FOR YOU

"Well, that's great, Jerry. But what does this have to do with me today?"

It has everything to do with you. According to Galatians 3:29 — *And if ye be Christ's, then are ye Abraham's seed, and* **heirs according to the promise.**

What is God saying? He is saying that it didn't end with Abraham. It didn't end with David. It didn't end with Solomon. Jesus came and broke the curse over mankind. He redeemed us from the curse and put us in position so that you and I can walk in the same blessing, the same increase, and the same favor. In fact, we should have it better than they had because our covenant is a better covenant founded upon better promises.

INCREASE IN YOUR LIFE IS YOUR RIGHT

God is interested in you increasing in every area of your life. Now, obviously, everyone would agree that God wants us to increase spiritually. The Bible says that when we get born again, we begin on the milk of God's Word so that we may grow thereby. And if you have been serving God a number of years and you haven't grown spiritually, then something is wrong. It's a violation of spiritual law. God expects you to grow spiritually.

He also expects you to grow where your soul is concerned. Your soul is made up of your mind, your will, and your emotions. The Bible talks about the prosperity of your soul in 3 John 2.

Prosperity of the soul would be your mind being renewed to the Word of God, your will being conformed to His will, and your emotions being under the control of God's Word. That is soulish prosperity, or, you could say increasing in the area of your soul.

And, of course, you should be increasing where your physical body is concerned also. And, I'm not talking about gaining weight! I'm talking about walking in a greater level of divine health. The Bible says, *He sent His Word and healed them* (Psalm 107:20). So if you are spending quality time in the Word, then it should have an effect on your physical well-being.

Now I am not saying that you will not ever have symptoms of sickness trying to come on you. I get symptoms from time to time, but I have learned how to take the Word of God and apply it to those symptoms, and then one of two things must happen. The Word of God must bow to the symptoms or the symptoms must bow to the Word of God. And, in my case, the symptoms bow every time. So enjoying better health is increasing physically. And that is part of God's plan.

So we know that we should increase spiritually, mentally (or soulishly), and physically. And God also expects as you serve Him and as you put His Word first place in your life, that there should be signs of financial increase.

For you to never experience financial increase in your walk with God is a violation of spiritual laws.

There is absolutely no way you can walk with God, keep His covenant, and not experience financial increase. It has to come. No, I didn't say it would come overnight. I didn't say it will come in a matter of days. What I did say is that it will come!

GET MAD

Now, once I realized my covenant rights as a child of God, I got mad. I went to my wife and said, "Carolyn, we are living beneath our privileges as covenant people. We have a covenant with God. We have a contract with the Almighty, the Creator of the universe." We got mad at the devil and we started acting on our covenant rights and things started to change in our lives.

The Creator of the universe has made a contract, a legal document with us. And in that contract, it says that we are redeemed from the curse of poverty. That means that we don't have to spend the rest of our lives living from paycheck to paycheck. We don't have to live the rest of our lives barely getting by, just existing, and just settling for whatever crumbs the devil will give us.

I quickly decided that I wanted God's blessing on my life. And I wasn't going to give up until I had it. A man asked me one time when he found out that I was going into ministry, he said, "Are you going to take a vow of poverty?"

I said, "No."

He said, "You're not?"

I said, "No. Why would I want to do that?"

"Well, don't you think preachers ought to be poor?"

"No. I think they ought to be blessed."

WHY DOESN'T HE SET THE EXAMPLE?

If God wanted us to live in poverty, then why wouldn't He set the example? Have you ever thought about that? If He loves poverty so much and wants His followers to live in poverty, then why doesn't He set the example?

It seems to me like the least He could do is set the example. But He doesn't live in poverty. My Bible talks about streets of gold. Have you ever read the description of the Throne Room? Trust me. God's not doing badly at all.

Think about what Jesus said. He said, *In my father's house are many mansions: ... I go to prepare a place for you...* (John 14:2). If God wanted us to live in poverty, then Jesus would have said, "In My Father's house are many shacks, and I will go repair one for thee."

My point is this: God doesn't love poverty. He considers it a curse. And you have been redeemed from that curse. God wants you to prosper in every area of your life and have good success.

DECLARE WAR ON YOUR FINANCIAL CONDITION

You have a right to increase. You have a right to have all of your needs met and plenty left over. It is your covenant right as a child of God to experience increase. And if you're not, then you need to declare a state of war on the devil today! You are being robbed!

Now, don't think this war is going to be easy. It's not. The devil is not just going to roll over and play dead. Trust me, the fight will be on. But you are the one that has weapons that are not carnal but mighty through God. You are the one that has God backing you. You are the one that God has promised that no weapon formed against you shall prosper. You can win this war. But you must be determined and persistent. You must not quit. Quitting cannot be an option.

My mandate since 1969 has been to talk people into winning, to teach them that God is a covenant-keeping God and that their covenant with Him is a covenant of increase. God wants you to increase. He wants you to have all your needs met and then have plenty left over. But, He wants you to do it His way. And that's why I am writing this book. To help you experience *increase God's way*.

"God's way? What are you talking about?" You may ask.

God has a way for you to experience increase in your life. He has laid it out in the Word. And I am going to show you in this book how to experience increase His way and with His blessing. So, get ready for increase to come into every area of your life.

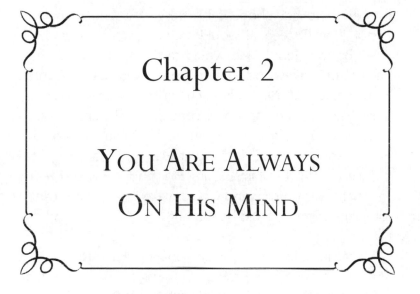

Chapter 2

You Are Always
On His Mind

Every once in a while I get a note from Dr. Oral Roberts. It will say something like, "Jerry, I just wanted you to know that I had you on my mind today. I'm praying for you." And then at the end it will say, "Something good is going to happen to you." Sometimes, he adds, "P.S. Carolyn is still prettier."

Those hand-written notes make my day. I just love getting personal notes like that from him. I mean, it just makes me smile a little bigger. Oral Roberts is thinking about me. That makes me feel special.

Don't you like it when you get unexpected notes from somebody saying that they were just thinking about you and praying for you? Or maybe it's a phone call from somebody. But, doesn't it make you feel special?

I used to get phone calls every now and then from Pastor John Osteen. I would answer the phone and say, "Hey, Brother John." He would say, "This is John Osteen, Pastor of Lakewood International Outreach Center, Houston, Texas." Now, I knew all of that but he would say it anyway. And then he would continue, "Just wanted you to know that Dodie and I had you on our mind this morning. Praying for you. Bye." And that was it. I wouldn't get a chance to talk. But him making that phone call and telling me that I was on his mind would make my day. It meant a lot to me that he would be thinking about Carolyn and me.

It means a lot to me when people call and tell me that they are thinking about me and praying for me. I like that. Well, what about our Heavenly Father? What is He thinking?

The Lord hath been mindful of us…

Psalm 115:12

Just reading that makes me excited. I wouldn't even have to read any further. Just knowing that God has me on His mind makes me excited. As much as I like getting notes and phone calls from other people telling me they are thinking about me, it doesn't begin to compare with knowing that God has me on His mind. I can make it through any day knowing that God has got me on His mind. And you can, too.

WHAT ARE YOU THINKING?

A lot of people believe that they are on the mind of God, but it's what they *think He is thinking* that is wrong. They think He is thinking of ways to hurt them, how He can put them down, or how He can make them sick, and so on and so on. But those are just lies from the devil. God is not the one who wants to make your life miserable. He is not the one who wants you sick. He is not the one who wants you in financial bondage for the rest of your life. The devil is the one who is out to steal from you, kill you, and destroy you. That is what he has on his mind when he thinks about you ... all day long.

But not God. God is thinking about life and giving it to you more abundantly.

The Lord hath been mindful of us: he will bless us...

Psalm 115:12

That's right. He's thinking about how He can bless you. That's what He is thinking right now. "How can I bless them? How can I manifest My favor on their behalf?" That's what's on His mind.

The Bible says that God never sleeps nor slumbers. So many times, when I go to bed at night I say, "Lord, I'm going to bed now and since you are going to be up all night, dream up new ways to bless me. I'll talk to you about it in the morning."

Right now, while you are sitting here reading this book, God has you on His mind. He is thinking about more ways that He can bless your life. Doesn't that make you feel good? That should bring a smile to your face no matter what your circumstances look like. He is thinking about how He can bless you!

BLESS, BLESS, BLESS, BLESS

...he will bless us; he will bless the house of Israel; he will bless the house of Aaron.

He will bless them that fear the Lord, both small and great.

Psalm 115:12-13

Notice how many times the word "bless" is used in those verses.

I have a commentary from Charles Spurgeon, the great preacher of old, called, "The Treasury of David." It's a commentary on all the Psalms.

Charles Spurgeon said, "The repetition of the word 'bless' shows that where God has once bestowed His favor, He continues it. His blessing delights to visit the same house often and to abide where it once lodged."

In other words, God wants His blessing to be upon your house not only right now but for the rest of your life.

HE'S GOT ENOUGH

Spurgeon went on to say, "It's God's nature to bless. It's His prerogative to bless. It's His glory to bless. And it is His delight to bless. Blessing us over and over and with more and more will not impoverish God."

Now, for some who may be reading this book, this is great news. You may be so far in debt that it looks as though there is no light at the end of the tunnel. Well, your need won't break God. If God supernaturally blessed every single person who reads this book beyond their wildest imaginations, it would not break Him. It wouldn't even make a dent in His capital reserve.

So don't ever think that your need is too big for God or that you are going to break Him. No. You can't break Him. He meets our needs according to His riches in glory by Christ Jesus. And those riches in glory are inexhaustible.

Spurgeon said this about the phrase ... *both small and great,* "So long as a man fears the Lord it matters nothing whether he be prince or peasant, patriarch or pauper. God will bless him."

So that should get rid of the thought that this only works for preachers. God has got you covered. You are just as much a child of God as I am or as anybody else is. So quit thinking: *I am just the little housewife. I am just the grocer. I am just the guy that works at the service station.* It doesn't matter. God wants to bless you no matter who you are or where you live or what you do. That has nothing to do with whether He can or will bless you or not. God keeps His covenant with His children. He is a covenant-keeping God.

MORE AND MORE

The Lord shall increase you more and more, you and your children.

Ye are blessed of the Lord which made heaven and earth.

Psalm 115:14-15

The very first part of that verse says that the Lord shall increase you. That's you He is talking about. He wants to bless YOU more and more. Not only that, He wants to bless YOUR CHILDREN.

And I can tell you as a parent, it's a joy to watch God bless your children. Both my daughters and their husbands have moved into brand new houses recently. God is not only blessing Carolyn and me, He is blessing our children. And He will bless my grandchildren as well.

That tells me that no matter where you are right now,

God has no problem with you increasing. Now, some sinners might have a problem with it. But God doesn't. I have found that the people who have the biggest problem with me being blessed are carnal-minded Christians. Religious people. They are the ones who have the biggest problem with increase. So don't be carnal-minded. Be Word-minded. Be covenant-minded!

WHY INCREASE?

Why does God want to bless you? Why does He want you living a life of divine prosperity? Because if you are, then your life becomes a testimony. Not only that, it becomes an attraction. It becomes an evangelistic tool.

When you are blessed and prospering when the economy is bad and when other people are being laid off, and yet you are prospering, eventually somebody is going to ask you what is going on. How are you doing this? Where are you getting it? And you can say, "I am blessed and highly favored by God."

That is the real reason that God wants you blessed. That's why He wants you to experience increase. Not just so you can live comfortably all of your life but so your life becomes an evangelistic tool.

I have won a lot of people to the Lord that I have never preached a word to. They just wanted to know about my lifestyle. "How are you doing this?" "Where are you getting this?" And I pointed to God. I told them that He was my source. My life makes God look good!

God has you on His mind. And now you know exactly what He's thinking about. He is thinking of ways that He can bless you. Ways that He can bless your children. Why? So your life will be an evangelistic tool that He can use. As long as you remember where the increase came from, then there is no limit to what God will do in your life. There is no limit to how much wealth, or increase, He will bring into your life.

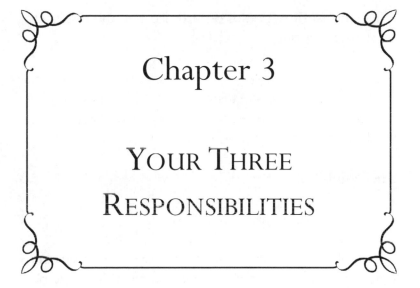

Chapter 3

Your Three Responsibilities

If somebody were to ask you what the wind looked like how would you answer? You probably wouldn't be able to tell them, but you would be able to describe the effects of the wind. Right?

When Carolyn and I were leaving our driveway recently, some trash was blowing across the yard. She stopped the car, and I got out and picked it up. Now, I couldn't see the wind. What I could see was the trash blowing around, the tree branches moving, and so on. I could see the effects of the wind, but not the wind.

The same is true about the blessing of the Lord. It is something that comes on your life. Blessed literally means empowered to prosper. So the blessing of the Lord is an empowerment that comes on your life, and the results can be seen by others.

Many times we call things like our cars or our house a blessing. It's okay to say things like that. But in reality, the house, the car, the clothes, and those kinds of things are the results of the blessing that is on you.

SEE THE RESULTS

"What are you talking about, Jerry?"

Carolyn and I recently kept several of our grandchildren. One night just before dark, I pulled out my 1932 Chevrolet Victoria and told the grandkids that we were going to go for a ride.

When I opened my garage door and my classic cars came into view, Carolyn said, "Now, this is a blessed garage."

And it is. God has blessed me. I say that unashamedly. I am a blessed man. But in reality, the things that have come into my life are a result of the blessing of the Lord that is on my life.

Now, let me show you some examples in the Word.

And Melchizedek king of Salem brought forth bread and wine: and he was the priest of the most high God.

And he blessed him (speaking of Abraham), *and said, Blessed be Abram of the most high God, possessor of heaven and earth:*

And blessed be the most high God, which hath delivered thine enemies into thy hand. And he gave him tithes of all.

Genesis 14:18-20

Notice that Melchizedek recognized that Abraham was blessed. There were results in his life that indicated the blessing of God was on him. In Genesis 24:1 it says, *And Abraham was old, and well stricken in age: And the Lord had blessed Abraham in all things.*

Once again, people knew there was something different about Abraham. And whatever it was produced phenomenal results. They found out that it was the blessing of God.

In fact, people literally sought out the blessing in Old Testament days. And there were some people who had no regard for it. Esau sold his blessing for food. It simply didn't mean to everyone what it should have.

Next, let's look at Isaac, Abraham's son.

And the man waxed great, and went forward, and grew until he became very great.

For he had possession of flocks, and possession of herds,

and great store of servants: and the Philistines envied him.

Genesis 26:13-14

Once again, there was something on Isaac's life that caused even his enemies to envy him. What was it? The blessing of God, an empowerment that came on his life.

As a matter of fact, if you'll read the first part of the story, there was a famine in the land, a drought. In today's terms we'd call it a bad economy. But even though there was a famine in the land, it did not affect the man on whom was the blessing of the Lord, Isaac. He sowed in the land, even though there was a famine, and the Bible says he received a hundredfold in the same year.

YOU *WILL* SUCCEED

If the blessing of the Lord is on you, you will succeed. It doesn't matter where you live. That has nothing to do with it. You can live in the darkest part of Africa or you could live in the biggest city in America, but if you are serving the Most High God and you are observing His Word and doing His Word, if you are meeting the requirements, then the blessing of the Lord will come on you and you will succeed. You will be prosperous and you will experience increase in every area of your life.

Remember the story of Lot and Abraham. It finally got to the point that Abraham had to tell Lot, "You choose which area you'd like to go to and whatever area you don't want, I will go to that area" (Genesis 13 – Author's paraphrase).

Lot, being the selfish and greedy man that he was, chose the area that looked to be the most fertile, the most industrious, and the area that looked to be the most prosperous. And Abraham went the other direction.

What happened to Abraham? God caused everything he set his hand to do to be blessed. Why? Because Abraham was empowered to prosper. The blessing of the Lord was on his life. So the circumstances didn't matter.

I have seen this happen in Africa many times. When I first went to Africa in the 1970s and started preaching these things – the blessing of the Lord, being the seed of Abraham, being redeemed from the curse – lives began to change. I went to places that were experiencing poverty. I am talking about mud huts, no electricity, no running water.

Now, I was told, "You can't preach prosperity here, Jerry."

"Why not?" I'd asked.

"Well, those people are poor."

"Yes. That's why I need to preach this. That is the reason God sent me here. To show them the truth."

And I did. I taught the same principles that I am sharing with you, and I can tell you that many of the people we ministered to ended up with nice homes, nice cars, their own businesses, and prospering. So it will work anywhere and for anyone who is willing to meet God's requirements.

Once again, God wants you to be blessed in every area of your life. That was His plan for mankind from the beginning, and it's His plan for His children today.

I want you to understand that the blessing of the Lord is an empowerment. It comes on your life, and the results of it can be seen by others. People may not know what to call it, but they know there's something different about you. They know there is something unusual and extraordinary about you. When the blessing of the Lord is on your life, it makes the God you serve look good, and it will draw people to Him.

PERMANENTLY HAPPY

I recently looked up the word "blessing" again and found that one of the meanings is to be *permanently happy*. I like that definition. Permanently happy.

How would you like to live your life permanently happy? That sounds good, doesn't it? Well, that's what happens when the blessing of the Lord is on you. The blessing of the Lord will bring permanent happiness into your life.

That means that no matter what kind of challenges you might be facing, no matter what kind of crisis you may be experiencing, no matter what may come your way, you are still happy and full of joy because the blessing of the Lord assures you that somehow, someway, God is going to turn your situation around and it's going to be all right.

CONTINUAL BLESSINGS

Now, when I saw "permanent happiness" that said to me that living a blessed life is something that God wants us to enjoy all the time, not just occasionally. I am not talking about a blessing here and a blessing there. I am talking about continual blessings.

"Well, Jerry, if that's true then why aren't more Christians living like that?"

The answer is because the promises of God are conditional. You could say that there are stipulations or require-ments to the promises of God. And these requirements must be observed.

The word "observe" means to give careful, heedful, and respectful attention to. This simply means that you are will-ing to give respectful attention to what God has said. And you are willing to obey it.

Jesus said it this way, *take heed to what you hear...*

Mark 4:24

The book of Revelation says several times, ... *He that hath ears let him hear... .* What is that saying? Pay careful attention. Take heed with respect. In other words, when you read the Word, do it respectfully.

Your Bible is not just another book. It is the Word of the Living God. It's called the Holy Bible for a reason. It is holy. But if you aren't careful, you can get to the place where it doesn't mean to you what it once did. Don't ever allow the Word of God to become just another book to you.

Let me encourage you today: if reading the Word or studying the Word has become casual to you, change how you look at it. Read it with respect and realize that the Creator of the universe is taking time to talk to you. That's what He's doing. Respect it and pay attention to what He is saying to YOU.

THE BIG "IF"

Once again, if you are going to become the recipient of a blessed life, then you need to observe the conditions to the promises of God.

And it shall come to pass, if thou shalt **hearken diligently** *unto the voice of the Lord thy God, to* **observe** *and to* **do** *all his commandments which I command thee this day…*

Deuteronomy 28:1

The first thing you should notice about that scripture is the word "if." That reveals a condition. These things will happen **IF**. The blessings will only happen IF you meet the requirements.

And what is required? The first thing you have to do is *listen* (hearken diligently) to what God is saying. Next, you must be willing to *observe*. That means you must give careful, respectful attention to. And lastly, you must *do* what He says.

It's not enough to just listen. It's not enough to just pay careful attention to what He says. You must then also do what He says.

The fact is that if you truly respect what He says, then there will be no problem with doing whatever He says to do.

The conditions: listen, observe, and do.

And all these blessings shall come on thee and overtake thee.

Genesis 28:2

OBEDIENCE

So God expects us to hearken diligently unto His voice and observe and do whatever He tells us to do.

Let me just say that God always blesses obedience. That means a blessed life is the result of an obedient life. Obedience is the act of submitting to God's commands. It's doing whatever God might ask you to do. Every person in the Bible who conducted their lives in a manner in which they were obedient lived a blessed life. And I believe He will do the same today.

Someone once asked Dr. Paul Yonggi Cho, pastor of the largest church in the world, what his secret to success was. Why was he so blessed? He simply replied, "I pray and I obey."

Oh, that's too easy. No. That's as profound as it gets. Find out what God wants you to do, hearken unto His voice, observe, and then do it.

If ye be willing and obedient, ye shall eat the good of the land.

Isaiah 1:19

If they obey and serve him, they shall spend their days in prosperity, and their years in pleasures.

Job 36:11

If you want to spend your days in prosperity and your years in pleasures, if you want the blessing of the Lord to come on your life, if you want increase His way, then obedience is a must.

IT'S ONLY A MATTER OF TIME

Therefore hear, O Israel, and be careful to observe it, that it may be well with you, and that you may multiply greatly as the Lord God of your fathers has promised you – a land flowing with milk and honey.

Deuteronomy 6:3 (New King James Version)

So it shall be, when the Lord your God brings you into the land of which He swore to your fathers, to Abraham, Isaac, and Jacob, to give you large and beautiful cities which you did not build,

houses full of all good things, which you did not fill, hewn-out wells which you did not dig, vineyards and olive trees which you did not plant – when you have eaten and are full –

then beware, lest you forget the Lord who brought you out of the land of Egypt, from the house of bondage.

Deuteronomy 6:10-12 (New King James Version)

lest – when you have eaten and are full, and have built beautiful houses and dwell in them;

and when your herds and flocks multiply, and your silver and your gold are multiplied…

Deuteronomy 8:12-13 (New King James Version)

Did you notice something about all of these verses? Notice God always says **when** these things happen. It doesn't say if it happens. He doesn't say that it might happen. As far as God is concerned, if you hearken diligently, observe, and do what He says, then it is <u>when</u> it happens. When increase comes in your life.

It's not a question to God, that if you will do what He says, whether you will increase. He says **when** it happens. So if you do what He says, then it's just a matter of time and increase is coming into your life. Once again, God is a covenant-keeping God. He keeps His Word. If you will fulfill your part, He'll always fulfill His.

THE RULES OF THE GAME

If you want the blessings of God to come on you and overtake you, then you must be willing to meet the conditions. If you are not willing to hearken, if you are not willing to observe, and if you are not willing to do what God says, then He is under no obligation to empower you to prosper.

That may seem pretty harsh, but it's true. God sets the rules.

God sets the rules that enable us to experience His blessing upon our lives. If we play by His rules, then we will increase.

Contrary to what you might have thought, the rules were not set by God to be a hardship on us. They weren't. And I can tell you that when I finally understood that, it made playing by His rules so much easier for me. At first I thought God was just being hard. I thought – *Why is He so demanding?* He sets these rules, makes us live by them, and then if we don't, we don't get to play. Doesn't seem fair, does it? It didn't seem fair to me anyway.

I later came to realize the reason God sets the rules is because once I meet them, it's not hard on me. It's hard on the devil. Once the conditions are met, then the pressure is on the devil, not you.

"What?" You may ask.

Once you meet the conditions that God sets, then God promises He will cause the results. Now, who has the pressure? Not me. Not you. The pressure is on the devil. And there is nothing he can do to stop the results if you meet the conditions. He simply cannot do it.

The Bible says, ...*Resist the devil, and he will flee from you.*

James 4:7

A higher power than you or me or the devil made that statement. God said it. He is saying that once you meet the conditions, then He will see to it that the devil flees.

Have you ever noticed that God did not make that promise to the devil? He never said to him, "If you will resist My people, they will flee." He never said that. The devil doesn't have that promise, but you and I do. If we resist him, he will flee.

Once again, yes, there are conditions, there are stipulations, and there are requirements, but they are not there to make it hard on us. They are there to make it hard on the devil.

So hearken diligently, observe, and do. IF you will do these things, then the blessings WILL come on you and overtake you. It's only a matter of time. And remember, God wouldn't ask you to do it if you couldn't. You can do it! You can do these three simple things and meet the requirements for experiencing increase God's way.

Chapter 4

THE HEART
OF THE MATTER

In the first chapter, I told you and showed you in the Word that it was God's original intent for you and me to live a blessed life. Or you could say a *prosperous* and *successful* life. And it's still His plan for His children today. He doesn't want you barely getting by. He doesn't want you living from paycheck to paycheck. No. He wants you blessed so that you can be a blessing. He wants you blessed so you can prevent misfortune in the lives of others. He wants you blessed so you help spread the life-changing message of Jesus Christ to a hurting and dying world. He wants you blessed in every area — physically, soulishly, spiritually, and financially. It's your covenant right.

Now, let's just be honest. I know that a lot of people think that as Christians we are supposed to be poor. And by being poor that somehow means that we are more spiritual. But that's a lie. It's just not true. And you can't find that anywhere in the Bible.

The truth is that when you are prosperous and success-ful you have more opportunities to influence people than when you are not. It gives you a greater voice. It makes the God you serve look attractive. Not only that, you can do more for the kingdom of God when you are prosperous and successful than when you are not.

Think of it this way. If your church was building a new building that would seat more people, which would you rather give – $25.00 or $2,500.00? Now, please understand that I am not saying anything bad about giving $25.00. If that is what you have and that's the best you can do, then do it, and God will honor it. But if you were living a life of divine prosperity and could give $2,500.00, isn't that being able to do more for the kingdom of God?

It's like I heard somebody say, "I once was rich and I once was poor, and rich is better."

Just think about what it would be like for you to not have to worry about paying your house payment this month or wondering how you are going to come up with the money to pay your electric bill. Wouldn't it be nice to go to the grocery store and just buy all the groceries that you need and want and not have to worry about it? That is what God wants for you. He wants you to be able to do all those things. His idea is that you have so much that you could pay for somebody else's groceries or make their house payment or pay their electric bill, and still not have to worry about it affecting your finances in any way.

THE ULTIMATE PURSUIT

Now, with all that being said, you must keep all of this in its proper perspective. God's intent is for you to be prosperous and blessed. However, He never intended for those things to be your #1 pursuit. God wants you to make **Him** your #1 pursuit. True prosperity and success are the results of having an intimate relationship with Him. So you must remember to seek Him first, not prosperity.

A lot of people have the idea that if they put God first then that means that they will never have anything. Once again, that's not true. That's religious thinking. Not the Bible. Jesus said, *But seek ye first the kingdom of God, and his righteousness; and all these things shall be added unto you* (Matthew 6:33). The "things" that Jesus was referring to were material things. The necessities of life. He simply wants to be #1 in your life. He wants following Him and getting to know Him intimately to be the #1 pursuit of your life. If it is, then there is no limit as to how far God will take you. There is no limit to how much He will bless you. It will be beyond what you could possibly ask or think.

GOOD SUCCESS

This book of the law shall not depart out of thy mouth; but thou shalt meditate therein day and night, that thou mayest observe to do according to all that is written therein: for then thou shalt make thy way prosperous, and then thou shalt have good success.

Joshua 1:8

I want to focus on the word "success." God says you will make your way prosperous and you will have good success. Notice that this is God speaking. He is the one who brought this up. Not Joshua. God told Joshua that if he would do certain things, then it would produce prosperity and success in his life.

In this book we are talking about increasing God's way. Prospering God's way. So if we are going to increase God's way, then we must do the things that He says will bring about prosperity and success in our lives.

WHAT IS SUCCESS ANYWAY?

As I was studying this, I began thinking about the word "success." *And thou shalt have good success.* So what is success and what does it truly mean?

You could ask a whole room full of people how they would define success, and I am sure there would be many answers. Some might say it means having more money than they could ever imagine. Somebody else might say it would mean never having to worry about paying their bills again. That would be success for some people. Still others might say that success is being able to retire at a very young age. For a different person it might be having peace in their minds and being happy on the inside.

To another person, success might mean tapping into their full potential. I heard a famous athlete once describe success as, "Doing the absolute best that you are capable of doing and having fun while you are doing it."

Once I heard a very well-known person say that success to him would be, "Being stimulated, being challenged, being inspired, and accomplishing what others say is impossible."

Somebody else might say that success actually has nothing to do with you. It's what you do for others that determines how successful you are.

GOD'S DEFINITION OF SUCCESS

My point is that there are many definitions as to what success actually is. But, God also has an opinion about success. He has His own definition of success. And His definition is the one that matters the most. Don't you agree?

I asked Him recently, "What is Your definition of success? What is success in Your eyes?"

Now, I must say, I was surprised at what scripture He led me to. Let me forewarn you. When you first read it, you will think, "What in the world does that have to do with success and increase in my life?" It's going to sound like it doesn't have anything to do with financial well-being, but it does. So here we go. Here's God's definition of success:

He hath shewed thee, O man, what is good; and what doth the Lord require of thee, but to do justly, and to love mercy, and to walk humbly with thy God?

Micah 6:8

Success to God is doing justly, loving mercy, and walking in humility.

SUCCESS IN GOD'S EYES

Now, as I began to pray and meditate that, what I heard the Spirit of God say was that living a life of integrity, loving mercy (or being compassionate toward others), and then walking humbly before God (or never forgetting that without Him you are nothing and always acknowledging Him as the source of everything good in your life) was being successful.

If you will do those things *consistently,* then God says you are a success. And consistently means being faithful.

What is success in the eyes of God:

1. Living a life of integrity

2. Being compassionate toward others

3. Walking humbly before God

4. Being faithful

Once again, I know right now that it doesn't seem like these characteristics have anything to do with financial increase in your life. But just stick with me. It does, and I'm going to show you how every one of these qualities will produce prosperity and success in your life.

When you possess these four characteristics in your heart, it will have a profound impact on your financial well-being. God richly blesses those who not only keep His Word but those that do His Word as well.

The world knows very little about these four qualities. As a matter of fact, not very many in the body of Christ know much about these things. But I assure you that they are the qualities that God looks for in a person. When He finds them, then there is no way Satan can keep that person from prospering and being successful. Why? Because God **always** honors His Word.

Integrity, compassion, humility, and faithfulness are issues of the heart. And let me say to you right now that nothing is more important to God than what's in a person's heart. What's in a person's heart is far more important to God than natural ability or natural talent.

LOOK TO THE HEART

God is interested in what is in a person's heart. Once again, integrity, compassion, humility, and faithfulness are matters of the heart. And that is what matters most to God. Even if you aren't extremely gifted or extremely talented, if your heart is right and these qualities are in your heart, then you'll have God's attention. You don't have to be the greatest orator or the most charismatic. God is looking for more than just natural gifts and talents.

We see this in the story of Samuel when he went out to anoint the next king of Israel.

But the Lord said unto Samuel, Look not on his countenance, or on the height of his stature; ... for the Lord seeth not as man seeth; for man looketh on the outward appearance, but the Lord looketh on the heart.

I Samuel 16:7

If you pay close attention to the story, you will see that when Samuel came to Jesse's house, Jesse lined up all his sons, except David. He didn't even bring him to the house. He left him out with the sheep. Why would he do that? Because in the mind of Jesse, David couldn't be the one. He didn't look like he was king material. He was just the shepherd boy.

But apparently it didn't bother David. He just stayed

out there with the sheep. In fact, after the ceremony was over, and after Samuel had said he was the one, David said, "Yes, sir. Thank you very much" (Author's paraphrase). And then he went right back to his sheep.

You know, if you feel as though there is absolutely no way that God can use you, and if you feel like you're not as talented or gifted as somebody else, don't worry about it. If you have these four qualities, then you have what God is looking for.

So once again, God is interested in what's in your heart. Increasing His way begins in your heart. It has very little to do with how you look or how smart you are. It's not about natural abilities. It has everything to do with the condition of your heart. God is looking for integrity. He is looking for people full of compassion. He is looking for humility and faithfulness.

HE'S GOT A GOOD HEART

Have you ever heard the statement – that man's got a good heart? We hear people say that about others all the time.

But what do people mean when they say that somebody has a good heart? What are they talking about? They are talking about integrity. They are talking about compassion. They are talking about humility. They are talking about faithfulness.

When people say somebody has a good heart, they are saying that he keeps his word. He shows love to others. He is not boastful. He acknowledges the goodness of God in his life and he is a faithful man.

As sad as it is to say, there are many people in the body of Christ, that want success and prosperity but they just don't have any character. They have no integrity. And that is sad. It shouldn't be that way. If there is any place that you ought to be able to find these qualities, it should be in Christians. People with these qualities are often hard to find.

ARE YOU A CANDIDATE?

My point is that God is not going to make an unlovely, never keeps his word, arrogant, unfaithful person wealthy. Why? Because the prosperity of a fool will destroy them. And a person who has no integrity, no compassion, no humility, and is unfaithful is a fool in the eyes of God. And prosperity in that kind of person's life would destroy them.

The Bible warns us that if you become prosperous and successful through deception, dishonesty, usury, and oppression, then your prosperity will not last.

Wealth gotten by vanity shall be diminished…

Proverbs 13:11

...will dwindle away.

Proverbs 13:11 (Amplified Bible)

One who increases his possessions by usury and extortion gathers it for him who will pity the poor.

Proverbs 28:8 (New King James Version)

This is the wealth transfer that the Bible talks about. The Bible is telling us that the person who is oppressing other people and getting wealthy from deception and unjust means will eventually turn his wealth over into the hands of those who have their hearts right.

However, Christians who have no integrity and are unfaithful, who don't walk in love, and are arrogant are not candidates for the wealth transfer.

...the wealth of the sinner is laid up for the just.

Proverbs 13:22

So if you are a person of integrity, if you walk in love, if you remain humble, and if you are faithful, then you are a candidate for true prosperity and success.

SUCCESS: GOD'S WAY –
SEE WHAT IT WILL PRODUCE FOR YOU

Once again, God's definition of success.

He hath shewed thee, O man, what is good; and what doth the Lord require of thee, but to do justly, and to love mercy, and to walk humbly with thy God?

Micah 6:8

Now, I said earlier that these qualities will produce financial increase in your life. Let me show you how from the Word.

Integrity – *The righteous man walks in his integrity; blessed (happy, fortunate, enviable) are his children after him.*

Proverbs 20:7 (Amplified Bible)

This tells me that the person who walks in integrity is not only blessed, but his children after him will be blessed as well. What does it mean to be blessed? Empowered to prosper! So, integrity does pay off.

Compassion – *That ye may walk honestly toward them that are without, and that ye may have lack of nothing.*

I Thessalonians 4:12

Walking honestly toward those that are without, or in other words, being compassionate to people who are in need, brings about *lacking nothing.* That is the reward for being compassionate. The Amplified Bible says it this way, *...eventually you will become dependent on nobody and have need of nothing.*

So God's way for you to prosper, or God's way for you to have your own needs met, is to get involved in the needs of others. Just walk compassionately (walk in love) toward other people, and God will see to it that you prosper and have good success.

Wouldn't you agree that having need of nothing and being dependent on nobody would be a good definition of prosperity? And that is what the Word of God promises.

Humility — *Therefore humble yourselves under the mighty hand of God, that He may exalt you in due time.*

I Peter 5:6 (New King James Version)

The word "exalt" means to elevate or to bring **increase.**

The reward of humility and the reverent and worshipful fear of the Lord is riches and honor and life.

Proverbs 22:4 (Amplified Bible)

Humility pays off.

Faithfulness – *A faithful man shall abound with blessings…*

Proverbs 28:20

Faithfulness pays off.

THE CHALLENGE

God's way to prosperity and success is integrity, com-passion, humility, and faithfulness. Now, I have just given you a few scriptures, but there are many more that reveal to us that all of these qualities pay off in the form of blessings, prosperity, success, and financial well-being.

There's nothing wrong with wanting to be successful or desiring increase in your life, but just do it God's way. Make God's definition of success your definition of success. When you do that, then increase will come into your life God's way. And when you do it His way, you'll have His blessing.

The blessing of the Lord, it maketh rich, and he addeth no sorrow with it.

Proverbs 10:22

So, let me challenge you today, make sure that integrity, compassion, humility, and faithfulness are characteristics in your heart. When they are, increase is going to come into your life God's way and with His blessing. And when God's blessing is on what you are doing, then it is going to have a profound impact on your financial well-being.

God is interested in you having good success. He just wants you to do it with a right heart!

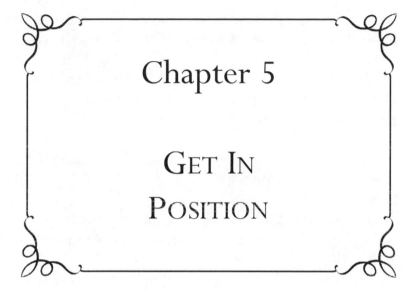

Chapter 5

GET IN POSITION

There are certain things that we must do to put ourselves in position to experience the increase that God wants us to have in our lives. And that is what I want to talk about in this chapter, getting in position to experience increase. God wants you to experience increase in your life. I have shown you that from His Word. Now I want to show you the various ways that are outlined in the Bible revealing how you and I can position ourselves to experience this increase.

#1. KEEP COVENANT

As long as God's people kept covenant with Him, increase came into their lives. They did not experience lack and financial bondage until they broke covenant. And that was what put them in bondage. He warned them in Deuteronomy 8:10-14:

When thou hast eaten and art full, then thou shalt bless the LORD thy God for the good land which he hath given thee.

Beware that thou forget not the LORD thy God, in not keeping his commandments, and his judgments, and his statutes, which I command thee this day:

Lest when thou hast eaten and art full, and hast built goodly houses, and dwelt therein;

And when thy herds and thy flocks multiply, and thy silver and thy gold is multiplied, and all that thou hast is multiplied;

Then thine heart be lifted up, and thou forget the LORD thy God, which brought thee forth out of the land of Egypt, from the house of bondage;

In Deuteronomy, specifically chapters 6, 8, and 28, it talks about keeping God's commands. God told them, **If you will keep covenant with Me, then My blessings will come on you and overtake you** (Deuteronomy 28:2). Right?

Now, if blessings are coming on you and overtaking you, then surely that would mean you are increasing. Wouldn't you agree? How could you not be increasing if blessings were continually coming on and overtaking you? Even if you gave it all away, you would still increase. Why? Because you cannot out give God. You simply can't do it. If you give to Him, He will give back to you good measure, pressed down, and shaken together (Luke 6:38).

In the literal Hebrew, one of the meanings of the word "overtake" is surprise. I like to say God is the God of surprises. If you will keep covenant with Him, then He will constantly surprise you with blessings.

And that is a good way to live, let me tell you. I love surprises and God is continually surprising me. As a matter of fact, whenever I come home from a meeting, Carolyn often says, "What did God surprise you with this time, Jerry?"

It's a great way to live. It's how God wants you to live. He wants to continually surprise you with His blessings.

#2. WALKING IN OBEDIENCE

Obedience is what opens the door to supernatural increase. God demonstrated this to His people time and time again.

Now, obedience is not only referring to the written Word but also to the specific word that God speaks to you as an individual. The little things that God talks to you about on a daily basis, you must be willing to obey them.

If the Lord tells you to buy your pastor's wife a new dress, then do it and do it quickly and quietly. Don't argue with God. Your attitude shouldn't be, "She doesn't need a new dress. Why does she need a new dress? That couldn't have been God." No, that's not obedience. Obedience is doing what you are told when you are told.

Isn't that how you want your children to obey you? Don't you want them to just do what you have told them to do and not argue with you or come up with a better plan? I know that is how Carolyn and I wanted our girls to obey us when they were growing up.

When our girls were young I found a verse in the Bible that said, "Children obey your parents quickly and quietly and it will be well with thee" (I Timothy 3:4). So I said, "All right girls, this is the way you are going to obey from now on. Quickly and quietly. That means you don't question it and that means you don't try to come up with a better idea. You just do it, quickly and quietly."

And I can tell you, from experience, that is how God wants us to respond to Him. One time I was having a discussion with our girls about obeying quickly and quietly, and I said, "Girls, I told you that the way you are going to obey is quickly and quietly, and when you don't, you are being disrespectful to me."

And God said to me, "I feel the same way."

I said, "Lord, I'm talking to my girls now."

He said, "Every time you refuse to act on what I tell you to do, then you are showing disrespect to Me."

Well, I quickly changed my attitude where my obedience to Him was concerned.

So once again, obedience will bring increase into your life. We talked about this in the last chapter, but I want to remind you again that, according to Job 36:11, if you will obey Him and serve Him, then you will spend your days in prosperity and your years in pleasures.

#3. PUTTING GOD'S WORD FIRST PLACE IN YOUR LIFE

Blessed is the man that walketh not in the counsel of the ungodly, nor standeth in the way of sinners, nor sitteth in the seat of the scornful.

But his delight is in the law of the Lord; and in his law doth he meditate day and night.

And he shall be like a tree planted by the rivers of water, that bringeth forth his fruit in his season; his leaf also shall not wither; and whatsoever he doeth shall prosper.

Psalm 1:1-3

God is saying that if you will give His Word first place and meditate in His Word by day and by night, then He will make your way prosperous. Everything you set your hand to do will prosper. And if everything your hand is doing is prospering, then once again, increase is coming into your life.

When you put God's Word first place in your life, it will create an image on the inside of your heart as to how He wants you to live. All of the scriptures I have shared with you about being blessed and prospering are meant to create an image on the inside of you. God's image for your life.

Now, if you can't see yourself living the way God says He has planned for you to live, then you need to spend more time in His Word. If you can't see it on the inside, then it will never be a reality in your life. God said to me several years ago, "If you can conceive it, then you can receive it." But the opposite is also true. If you can't conceive it, then you can't receive it.

For the Lord your God is bringing you into a good land, a land of brooks of waters, of fountains and springs, flowing forth in valleys and hills;

A land of wheat and barley, and vines and fig trees and pomegranates, a land of olive trees and honey;

A land in which you shall eat food without shortage and lack nothing in it ...

Deuteronomy 8:7-9 (Amplified Bible)

Now, can you imagine lacking nothing? That is how God wants you to live. Lacking nothing. But if you can't imagine it, if you can't conceive living your life that way, then once again, it will never become a reality.

So what must you do? Spend more time in the Word. I like to say, your heart is the canvas, the Word of God is the oil, and the Holy Spirit is the artist. If you will spend enough time in the Word, then the Holy Spirit will paint an image on the canvas of your heart as to how God wants you to live, or in other words, His plan for your life. Once you see it on the inside, then it's just a matter of time and it will manifest on the outside. But it all begins with putting God's Word first place in your life.

#4. HARD WORK

Hard work and diligence. You don't hear those words very often. And I know that some people won't like hearing this, but it is still one of the ways in which we position ourselves for increase to come into our lives.

Some folks just want to sit at home and pray that money will rain down on them from heaven. I can tell you it's never worked that way for me. And I can't find that in the Bible anywhere. What I do find is that God blesses hard work. Norvel Hayes once said, "God doesn't bless lazy Christians." And that's true. God believes in hard work.

For a dream comes through much effort…

Ecclesiastes 5:3 (New American Standard)

Increase is not going to just show up if you don't do anything.

The Lord shall command the blessing upon thee in thy storehouses, and in all that thou settest thine hand unto...

Deuteronomy 28:8

Notice that God will command the blessing of the Lord on what you set your hands to do. How can He bless you if your hands are always in your pockets, doing nothing? He can't. Your hands have got to be busy doing something.

He becometh poor that dealeth with a slack hand: but the hand of the diligent maketh rich.

Proverbs 10:4

The person who has a slack hand ends up how? Poor. Another word for "slack" is idle, or doing nothing. That person ends up poor. But, on the other hand, the person whose hands are diligent, or busy, ends up rich. Increase comes to that person.

I remember my Dad telling me when I was growing up, "A man that doesn't work, doesn't eat." And I believed him. So when I went into the ministry, I didn't just sit around and pray all the time. That would have been ridiculous. I had an electric bill that I had to pay. I had a mortgage. I had two babies that I had to feed. What did I do? I worked. I worked at a TG&Y warehouse driving a forklift for $1.90 an hour, and I did other jobs. I said, "Lord, as far as I am concerned, I am in the ministry and I see myself as a preacher, but until this ministry is in a position to sustain me financially, I will do whatever it takes." And I did. I did a lot of jobs. Why? Because I needed to. If I hadn't, I would have lost what little I had. What happened? God blessed the work of my hands. He blessed my hard work and my diligence.

Now, what you have to be careful of is that you do not become dependent on yourself and what you can do with your hands only. Don't ever get to the place where you think you are "self-made." I can tell you, God is not very appreciative of that attitude. The fact is that if it wasn't for God, you wouldn't have hands. It takes the work of your hands and God blessing the work of your hands. God said, *...but thou shalt remember the Lord thy God: for it is he that giveth thee the power to get wealth...* Deuteronomy 8:18

Let's look at a few more scriptures that show us that God will bless what you do with your hands.

The hand of the diligent will rule...

Proverbs 12:24 (Amplified Bible)

That simply means that the person who is diligent will not be mastered by poverty. He'll overcome it. What happens when you overcome poverty? Increase comes.

Wealth gained by dishonesty will be diminished, But he who gathers by labor will increase.

Proverbs 13:11 (New King James Version)

... the soul of the diligent shall be made rich.

Proverbs 13:4 (New King James Version)

People who work hard will become a candidate for increase in their lives. Hard work and diligence is one of the ways in which God has established for us to experience increase in our lives. So if you want to experience increase, quit complaining, and get to work!

#5. GIVING TO GOD

Honoring God with your finances is one of the scriptural ways in which you experience increase.

Honour the Lord with thy substance, and with the firstfruits of all thine increase: So shall thy barns be filled with plenty...

Proverbs 3:9-10

Notice it says barns. Not barn. Barns. God wants you so blessed that it takes barns to hold it all.

How do you honor God with your finances? By tithing, first of all. God never intended for tithing to be a debt you owe. He meant it to be a seed that you sow. But He still expects you to do it. Why? Because it's a matter of respect. You do it out of respect for Him and everything that He has done in your life.

When I think of how God has blessed me and everything that He has brought into my life and done for me, I cannot imagine not giving back to Him. It would simply be rude, ill-mannered, and disrespectful. I am what I am today because of God and what He has done in my life.

I remember what my life was like before 1969. I proved what I could do. I was failing at everything. I remember that guy. I have memories of him and I have memories of his lifestyle, but when I remember him, it almost seems like it was somebody else's life. Not mine. My life today doesn't resemble that life at all. God has blessed me. God has favored me. God has brought increase into my life. And for me to not give back to Him after everything He has done for me would be disrespectful and dishonorable. He would have every right to fold His hands and say, "You've seen all the increase you are going to see until you get an attitude of gratitude."

Honoring God with your finances is really an issue of the heart. You should honor God with your finances because of what He has done for you. And I think we can all look at our lives and say that God has been good to us. Can't you? Just think about everything that He has done for you? Your thankfulness to Him for what He has done in your life should cause you to honor Him with your money.

There is one who scatters, yet increases more: And there is one who withholds more than is right, But it leads to poverty.

Proverbs 11:24 (New King James Version)

What does that mean? It means that the person who is always sowing (always scattering seed), the person who is always giving and honoring God with their finances, will increase. But it also means that the person who does not, the one who is withholding when he should be sowing, will eventually end up in poverty. And it goes on in verse 25 to say that the generous person will be made rich and he who waters will also be watered.

Now that's a great way to live. You water others, and in the process, you always get watered. How do you get to that place? By honoring God with your finances.

Now, I have heard people say, "Well, as soon as my ship comes in, I'm going to really give big to God." The problem with that is that most people who say those things have never sent a ship out. Not only that, you can't wait for perfect conditions to start sowing. You have to start honoring God with your finances where you are. Once again, don't look at it as a debt you owe, but a seed you sow. Do it because you have an attitude of gratitude.

Keeping covenant, walking in obedience, putting God's Word first place in our lives, hard work and diligence, and honoring God are ways that **WE** put ourselves in position to experience God's increase in our lives. If you don't get into position, you will miss out on what God wants you to have. You will miss out on the life that He has planned for you. Now, you might experience a blessing here and there, a financial breakthrough here and there, but that's not God's best for you. Your covenant with Him is a covenant of increase. He wants you continually increasing. He wants you to have **barns** full. He wants you to live in divine prosperity, not just experiencing occasional breakthroughs. So let me encourage you today to get in position for increase. You will never regret it.

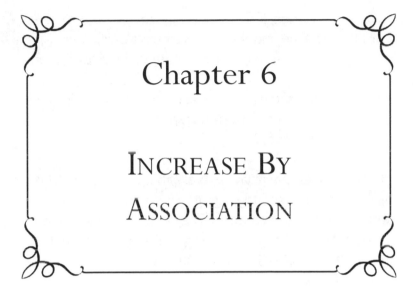

Chapter 6

Increase By Association

Birds of a feather do what? They flock together.

What happens in the secular world when there is a person who is successful in their business? What happens? People want to associate with them. They want to learn the secrets of their success, right?

I have a book that was given to me several years ago called "Uncommon Friends." It's not a spiritual book. But I enjoy this book so much that I read it every two or three years. It inspires me.

The book is about the relationship Thomas Edison, Henry Ford, Harvey Firestone, Alexis Carrel and Charles Lindbergh had. These great entrepreneurs were all friends. Not only were they friends, they bought houses together in

Fort Myers, Florida, just so that they could come together from time to time and throw ideas out at each other. They would get together, hang out, associate, and pick one another's brains. How would you have liked to have been a fly on the wall in that setting and be able to listen to them? Just think about it. These men are responsible for a lot of how we live our lives today.

There is a spiritual law at work that the body of Christ, by and large, knows little about. The world understands it better than the church does. They may not understand it's a biblical principle, but they do understand the concept and the results that it brings. What is that spiritual law? Increase by association.

Who you associate with has everything to do with your destiny and everything to do with the outcome of your life. It also has everything to do with what kind of increase you will experience in your life.

My best friends, the people that I run with, my buddies, are not "losers." They are not people who go around talking defeat all the time. They don't go around having pity parties when things aren't going like they planned. No. They are winners. They have a positive attitude. They don't accept defeat in their lives.

Why do I associate with these kind of people? Why are these kind of people my buddies? Because there is a spiritual law at work.

He who walks with wise men will be wise, But the companion of fools will be destroyed.

Proverbs 13:20 (New King James Version)

The Message Translation says it this way:

If you run around with fools or people who don't act wisely, watch, your life will fall apart.

That's strong. What do you suppose will happen to you if the only people you ever associate with are ones who believe that God wants you to be poor? Guess what? You will stay poor. But what happens if you walk with wise men? You will increase in wisdom. It's the spiritual law of increase by association, and we see it all over the Bible.

You see it in Moses and Joshua. Moses was told by God to lay his hands on Joshua, his servant, and his spirit would come on him (Numbers 27). He was telling Moses that the wisdom He had given him would come on Joshua. Joshua's association with Moses caused the same anointing, the same wisdom, the same leadership skills to come on him.

You see it in Elijah and Elisha. Elijah was a powerfully anointed man of God and because of Elisha's association with him, that same anointing and more came on Elisha. He wanted, and received, a double portion of the anointing that was on Elijah's life. But it all began with a spiritual link or you could say *hookup*.

What about Laban and Jacob?

And Laban said unto him, I pray thee, if I have found favour in thine eyes, tarry: for I have learned by experience that the Lord hath blessed me for thy sake.

Genesis 30:27

Laban is telling Jacob that the reason he is blessed is because he (Jacob) had come into his life. God blessed Laban because of his association with Jacob.

Another example is Jesus and the disciples. At least the one's who decided to become partakers of it. It was available to all of them, but not all of them benefited from it. Peter did. John did. What did it bring about for them? Increase. How? By association with Jesus.

After Jesus was raised from the dead, He ascended to His Father. His Father said, *"All power has been given unto me both in heaven and in earth,"* and then He gives it to Jesus. What does Jesus do? He then comes back into the earth and gives it to His disciples. He returns to heaven and takes His position at the right hand of God.

The next thing you know, you see Peter in the book of Acts acting just like Jesus did. As a matter of fact, if you hadn't known better, you would have thought it was Jesus. Peter acted just like Him. That same anointing worked through him just like it did in Jesus.

There was a time in Jesus' ministry when He went to raise a little girl from the dead. What was the first thing He did when He got there? He ran all the unbelief out of the house. He got all the unbelieving relatives out so He could minister faith to this little girl.

In the book of Acts, you see Peter doing the same thing. One of the first things he did was run all the unbelief out and the same anointing that was on Jesus was administered by Peter. What is that? Increase by association.

Do you know what a Christian really is? Christ means "anointed One." A Christian is a "little anointed one." The association that we have with Jesus should be producing the same anointing in our lives that worked in Jesus' life.

Look at what the Apostle Paul wrote about this spiritual law.

I thank my God upon every remembrance of you,

Always in every prayer of mine making request for you all with joy,

For your fellowship in the gospel from the first day until now,

Philippians 1:3-5 (New King James Version)

That word "fellowship" is also translated partnership or association.

Being confident of this very thing, that He who has begun a good work in you will complete it until the day of Jesus Christ;

Just as it is right for me to think this of you all, because I have you in my heart, inasmuch as both in my chains and in the defense and confirmation of the gospel, you all are partakers with me of grace.

Philippians 1:6-7 (New King James Version)

Paul is saying that because of this relationship that they had with him from the very beginning of his ministry that the same grace that was on him was now on them.

Remember that this is the man to whom Jesus said, "My grace is sufficient." In other words, what Jesus told him was, "Paul, no matter what situation you find yourself in, My grace is sufficient to deliver you and to meet your need."

Time and time again throughout the book of Acts we see where Paul comes under attack. He is being challenged. He is experiencing adversity, and what happens? That grace that was on him, kicks in so-to-speak, and brings him out and delivers him. In fact, they couldn't kill him until he was satisfied that he had finished his course. When he was satisfied, He said, "I'm ready now. Do what you want with this body. I have accomplished everything that God has called me to do because His grace was sufficient" (Author's paraphrase).

And Paul tells the Philippian church, his partners, that because of their association with him, that they were partakers of that same grace. And then he says to them, *But my God shall supply all your need according to his riches in glory by Christ Jesus* (Philippians 4:19).

You know, there are a lot of Christians going around and confessing that scripture, but they are really not entitled to it. That scripture was birthed out of an association. It was not just to every Christian. It was inspired by the Holy Spirit for the people who had entered into a scriptural association with God's servant. Paul was writing to his partners. He was writing to the people to whom he had ministered and they appreciated what he had taught them. They appreciated the spiritual growth that had come into their lives. And today, Philippians 4:19 is to every Christian who will act upon this principle of giving just as they did.

Some theologians say that by the time Paul wrote this letter to the Philippian church, he had been in ministry anywhere from 10 to 30 years. Regardless if it was 10 years or 30 years, these people had been associated with him from the very beginning. If it was as small as 10 years, then you are still talking about a 10-year association with him. That is almost unheard of in the body of Christ today. For the most part, people don't honor the divine associations that God creates for them.

Many times, God creates a supernatural hookup or link in people's lives, and they are so insensitive that they don't recognize that it is a divine appointment and that God is endeavoring to bring more increase into their lives.

I have seen this principle work time and time again in my own life. I believe that because of my association with Kenneth Copeland, the spirit of prosperity that is on him has come on me. Because of my relationship and association with the late Kenneth Hagin, the same spirit of faith that was on him came to my own life. Because of my relationship and association with Oral Roberts, the anointing for healing and miracles has come on me.

I believe that when people partner with me, the same favor of God that's on me comes on them. And I receive testimonies daily confirming that.

The Word that Kenneth Copeland, Kenneth Hagin, and Oral Roberts preached changed my life. From the very beginning of my hearing their teachings and 38 years later I am still associated with them. I'm still a partner with every one of them. Even though Kenneth Hagin is now with the Lord, I still sow into his ministry. He who walks with the wise will be wise. It's a spiritual law. And increase by association is one of the avenues in which God intends to increase His children more and more.

Now, let me say this. You might be thinking, "Well, that's great for you, Jerry, but I don't know any of those people. They are your friends. You know them personally. I will never get that opportunity."

Let me tell you that you don't have to know them personally to be associated with them. You don't have to have breakfast with T. L. Osborn, lunch with Kenneth Copeland, and dinner with Oral Roberts in order to associate with them. You can associate with them by studying their materials. That constitutes a relationship. When you are receiving from their books and from their CDs, then that creates an association.

Let me give you an example of how this principle has worked through my own ministry.

Years ago a lady came and introduced herself to me at a meeting I was conducting. She told me that she wanted to sow into my ministry and all she had was one dollar, and it was her last dollar. I said, "Ma'am, I can't take this. It's your last dollar."

She said, "You don't believe what you preach, do ya, boy?"

I said, "Well, yes I do."

Then she said, "Then you should take my dollar so I can reap like you talked about in your sermon."

So I did. And she faithfully sent me a dollar every month for many years.

Years later, her daughter came to me one night and said,

"I just wanted to tell you what my mom's sowing into your ministry has produced. Mom recently died. She lived on a farm. What we didn't know at the time was that this was prime real estate. We sold her farm and it produced an enormous amount of money and made me a wealthy woman." She went on to say that she attributed this to her mom's partnership with my ministry.

Once again, that's increase by association. This little lady had faithfully sown into my ministry for years, and it produced financial increase in her daughter's life. Increase by association.

IT'S ALL ABOUT THE SOIL

In the teachings of the sower sows the word in Mark 4, you will notice that the sower sowed on four different occasions, but he only benefited from one. Why? Because the other three places he sowed were not proper soil. Three out of four times he didn't get his seed in the right kind of soil.

So it is not just sowing that brings increase, it's making sure that you get it in the right soil. And that is why partnership with the right ministries is so important.

One day as I was sitting in Oral Roberts' office, he said, "The Lord has impressed upon me to redirect my giving." He said, "I have been giving to a lot of ministries over the years. But I began to notice that I wasn't getting the kind of harvest that I used to get, and I questioned God, and I said, 'Why am I not getting the same kind of returns or even greater?'"

"God's reply to me was, 'Because some of the soil that you have been sowing into is no longer good soil.' He said, 'Redirect your sowing. Redirect your giving. Make sure you get your seed in soil that is productive. Put it in ministries of integrity. Put it in ministries with character. Redirect it.'"

That really spoke volumes to me. My ministry tithes 10% of its income to other ministries all over the world. So I started looking at some of the ministries that I was sowing into and that I had become partners with.

I discovered that some of the ground had become corrupted. One missionary I had supported for years wasn't building churches anymore. He took all the money and built himself a large house.

I found out that a minister friend of mine had been supporting this same man. I called him, and I said, "You need to send a representative to that nation, take a look at where your money is going. There's no church in that community where this man said he was going to build a church, but he's got a nice three-story home, and he is sending his kids to private school."

What happened? My seed was not going into good soil, and, consequently, it wasn't producing 30-, 60-, and 100-fold.

When Brother Roberts said what he did about redirecting his giving, I thought to myself, "He's talking about the difference between *throwing* seed and *sowing* seed." You can just throw your seed out there or you can sow it on purpose in the right kind of soil.

THE BEST SEED

When I was a little boy, my grandfather lived in Mississippi, and he was a farmer. It was how he made it through the depression when my dad was a kid. He had his own farm and he raised cattle and hogs. He grew vegetables and sold them at the market.

I watched my grandfather work the soil. He was so particular about how he worked it and got it prepared for receiving the seed. And he would talk to me about it. I would get on the back of the tractor, go to the field with him, and ask him questions.

I remember one time I said, "Grandpa, why is it that when the corn comes in you always get the best stalks and you put them in the barn, and then you take the second best and sell it at the market, and we eat the third best?"

I said, "Why don't we eat the best corn?"

He said, "No, Son. You don't eat the best corn. You save that for sowing for next year. If we started sowing that third best corn, just think what our crop would be like next year? It would just keep degenerating."

The same is true with you and me in our financial sowing. You save your best seed for sowing. Don't consume your best seed. Sow it. And sow it into good soil. Don't just throw it. Sow it into ministries of integrity and watch how God will cause it to produce a maximum harvest.

WALK WITH THE WISE, BE WISE

Walk with wise men and you will be wise. Increase by association is a spiritual law. And it is one of the ways that God wants to bring increase in every area of your life.

I believe that a lot of people get *talked into* breaking association when they are right on the verge of a major breakthrough. They leave too soon. They quit. And the reason the pressure was on them to leave is because Satan knew that a major breakthrough was coming. So he did everything he had to do to get them out of position for that breakthrough.

Birds of a feather flock together. Let me challenge you today to take a long hard look at who you are associating with. It has everything to do with you fulfilling your God-given destiny, and it has everything to do with experiencing increase in your life.

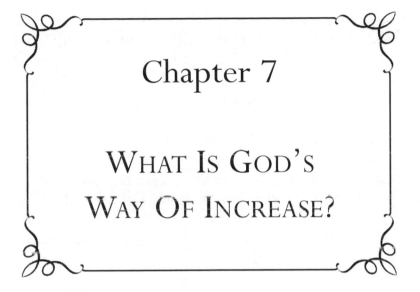

Chapter 7

What Is God's Way Of Increase?

"Oh, Brother Jerry, I just don't know. I just don't know that this will work. You don't understand. My family has always been poor. We have always been in debt."

"I don't have the right education."

"I don't have the right skin color."

"I don't live in America."

"I understand that God wants me blessed. I just don't think it can happen to me. I just don't know that I can ever experience the kind of increase that you are talking about."

Well, I can tell you this. I know it can work. I know it does work. I know that if you will do the things that I have shared with you, if you will listen, observe, and obey, get your heart right, and get in position to experience God's increase in your life, it WILL happen.

"How, do you know, Jerry?"

I know because I am living proof. I am living proof that it works. And if it will work for me, then it will work for you. God is no respector of persons. You just have to believe it and do it. The rest is up to God. And He never fails.

As for God, His way is perfect; The word of the Lord is proven…

2 Samuel 22:31 (New King James Version)

Now, I don't know about you, but that tells me that if I discover God's ways and then I put them to work, they will work every time. This scripture guarantees it. Why? Because God's ways are perfect. What do I mean by perfect? Without flaw. God's ways are without flaw.

DO YOU BELIEVE IT?

If you will discover God's ways, put them to work in your life, and not give up or quit, then God promises that His ways are perfect and His Word is proven. What does *His Word is proven* mean? It means that it has stood the test of time. God's Word has stood the test of time. It works every time that it is properly put to work.

"Yeah, but I've known people that acted on it and it didn't work. How do I know it will work for me?"

Well, you either believe what others have told you or you believe what the Word says. It's just that simple. If I were you, I'd pick the Bible.

"But what about their bad experience?" I don't know. But I do know that I will not base my faith on somebody else's experience. I am going to base my faith on "It is written." I have to. Why? Because people are capable of making mistakes, but God's way is perfect.

I had a man say to me one time, "Well now, wait a minute, Brother Jerry. You said God's ways are perfect, but let's remember He used a man to write that and how do we know he wrote it right?"

My reply was that anybody who could stand in the midst of total darkness and say two words — LIGHT BE! and light was, and 16 billion miles of universe was created, I am confident that He can get a man to write exactly what He wants them to write and get it right. Wouldn't you agree?

Once again, according to the Bible, God's ways are perfect and His Word is proven. Those are two very powerful statements, and if you can believe that, if you can get that down into your spirit, then you will never again ask: "What if it doesn't work?" That question will be a thing of the past for you.

I don't ask that question anymore. Now I did back in 1969. I wondered, "What if it doesn't work?" But it did work. Time and time again it has worked for me. His Word is proven. He has a wonderful track record in my life. He has never disappointed me. He has never failed me. Therefore, I believe I will stick to His way for my life. Why? It's perfect.

THE KINGDOM OF GOD

If you will approach life doing things God's way, then you will get God's results. This is exactly what Jesus was talking about in Matthew 6:33 when He said, *But seek ye first the* **kingdom of God,** *and his righteousness; and all these things shall be added unto you.*

The first thing you need to understand about that scripture is that the kingdom of God is not a place. The kingdom of heaven is a place. The kingdom of God is about principles. They are His ways.

What Jesus was saying in Matthew 6:33 was that if you and I will make it a priority in our life to seek, discover, and do God's way, then everything we need while we're on this planet will be added to us.

The Amplified Bible says that if you will … *aim at, and strive after… His way of doing and being right …*

The bottom line is if you will put God's ways as priority in your life (seek after, aim at, discover, and put them to work), then everything you will ever need while you are on this planet will be added unto you.

And when things are added unto you that means increase has come. What are we talking about? Experiencing increase God's way.

THE REAL QUESTION

God's ways are perfect. They work every time they're put to work. It's not a theory. It doesn't say, "God's way is a theory." No. It's perfect. James referred to it as "the perfect law of liberty."

So the real question is not: "Do God's ways really work?" The real question is: "Are you doing things God's way?"

In other words, if you are doing things God's way, then God says you will get His results because His ways are perfect and they are proven.

I like to say it this way: SEEKING HIS WAY + DOING HIS WAY = HIS RESULTS.

It's no wonder the psalmist said in Psalm 27:11 (Amplified Bible), *Teach me your way... .* So that should be the cry of our hearts today. Lord, teach me Your ways.

And if that is the cry of your heart, I can tell you that God will honor it. He did it for me and I was just an average guy. I came right out of a paint and body shop. I was as blue collar as you could possibly get. But, "Lord, teach me Your ways," became my heart's cry, and God has done just that. Like I said before, my life today doesn't even resemble my old life. So if it can happen to me, then it can happen to you.

AN INTERESTING THOUGHT

Now, here's an interesting thought for you. The psalmist said, *teach me your ways* .... I would like to submit to you that this is one of the reasons why Jesus came into the earth.

Who better to teach us God's way than *The Way* Himself? Jesus said it was one of His names. He said, "I am The Way."

Now you might be thinking, "Well, that was for His disciples in those days. I mean, you know, Jesus is at the right hand of God now. I know that He taught the disciples the ways of God, but what about us?"

Listen to what Jesus said.

These things have I spoken to you while being present with you.

But the Helper, the Holy Spirit, whom the Father will send in My name, He will teach you all things, and bring to your remembrance all things that I said to you.

John 14:25 (New King James Version)

Jesus is saying that it didn't end with those disciples. It didn't end with their generation. He said, "I am leaving. I am going to the Father. But I am going to send you another helper who is just like Me. And, in fact, the Helper I am going to send is not only going to be with you, He's going to move down on the inside of you. And He is going to take everything that I know and He is going to teach it to you" (Author's paraphrase).

If you are filled with the Holy Spirit, then you are totally unlimited. You have the teacher on the inside of you. And if anybody knows the ways of God, it's the Holy Spirit. And His assignment from Jesus Himself is to take what He knows about God's ways and reveal them to you.

Nevertheless I tell you the truth. It is to your advantage that I go away; for if I do not go away, the Helper will not come to you; but if I depart, I will send Him to you.

John 16:7 (New King James Version)

However, when He, the Spirit of truth, has come, He will guide you into all truth; for He will not speak on His own authority, but whatever He hears He will speak; and He will tell you things to come.

He will glorify Me, for He will take of what is Mine and declare it to you.

John 16:13-14 (New King James Version)

That simply means that if you and I will cry out, like the psalmist did, "Teach me, Lord, Your ways," then we are candidates for learning the ways of God. And if we learn them and do them, then we will never struggle with defeat again.

I did not say that you would never have adversity again. I said that you will never be defeated again because His ways are perfect.

Chapter 8

LIVE IT!

Increase. I have said throughout this book that God wants you to experience increase, in every area of your life. Increase is your covenant right. It doesn't matter if you are in debt right now. It doesn't matter if your bank account says zero. Increase is what God says is in store for you. It's His plan for your life.

So don't be discouraged by what might be happening right now in your life. It's not permanent. It's all subject to change.

While we do not look at the things which are seen, but at the things which are not seen. For the things which are seen are temporary, but the things which are not seen are eternal.

2 Corinthians 4:18 (New King James Version)

Back in 1974, as I was preaching in Gaston, Alabama, at a Full Gospel Businessmen's Convention, I got up to speak and the Lord lead me to 2 Corinthians 4:18. And when I saw *things which are seen are temporary,* all of a sudden the Lord said to me, "Son, that means subject to change." That exploded in my spirit. After I got through preaching, Kenneth Copeland came up behind me, hit me on the arm, and said, "Boy, why didn't you tell me that years ago?"

I said, "Well, I just found it out myself this morning."

I can tell you that when the Lord said that to me, it became a powerful revelation to me. And it became the foundation for maintaining my confidence in situations that looked permanent.

Every time I have faced something that looks immovable, that scripture comes up in my spirit. I can't begin to tell you how many times I have taken that one verse and stood on it. Having done all to stand, I stood on that verse. And it has worked every time. Not once in a while. Not a few times. It has worked every time.

So don't count yourself out even if your situation doesn't look as though increase is in your future. If you can see it, it's subject to change. Whatever it is that you are going through may look permanent, but if you can see it, it's not. It's subject to change.

This may come as a great surprise to you, but that is

how Jesus saw situations. That is exactly what He was talking about in the 11th chapter of Mark when He was talking about speaking to the mountain.

For verily I say unto you, That whosoever shall say unto this mountain, Be thou removed, and be thou cast into the sea; and shall not doubt in his heart, but shall believe that those things which he saith shall come to pass; he shall have whatsoever he saith.

Mark 11:23

Now Jesus was talking about a real, physical mountain. It wasn't a figure of speech like some people believe. No. He was talking about a mountain. He said, "Do you see that mountain? If you believe in your heart and do not doubt, then whatever you say shall come to pass. You can speak to this mountain, and it will be removed" (Author's paraphrase).

What is He saying? If you can see it, then it's subject to change. It's temporary. Therefore, don't give up just because your circumstances look as though they are permanent. They aren't.

Now, I've never had a reason to go speak to an actual mountain and tell it to move. I have never had a physical mountain stand in my way to experiencing God's best, but I have had some other kinds of mountains. Haven't you?

We even say phrases like, "My debts are <u>mounting</u> up." Or "I've got a mountain of debt."

But if you can see it, then it's not permanent, it's temporary. Whatever you are going through right now that might be preventing increase in your life, then it's subject to change.

Jesus even proved this with death. He proved that death was subject to change. You know, dead sounds permanent. Just think about it. When you look in a coffin and see a dead person in there, that looks permanent. It looks final. It's over.

But it wasn't in the mind of Jesus. He had a friend named Lazarus, and Lazarus died. By the time Jesus showed up, he had been dead for four days. Now, that's dead. In fact, the Bible even says that he stunk. So here is Lazarus. He is dead and he stinks.

And then Jesus comes on the scene. What does He do? He walks up to the tomb. And of course, Lazarus' sisters are there, and they are crying. They're all upset. Why? Because they think their brother's death is permanent. They saw his body. They knew he was dead. And they said to Jesus, "We all know that in the great resurrection, he'll rise again" (Author's paraphrase).

Jesus said, "I am the resurrection."

In other words, Jesus was taking it out of the sweet by and by and bringing it to the right now. He was about to prove that things which are seen are subject to change.

He said, "Lazarus, come forth."

What happened? Lazarus came forth proving that even death itself is subject to change.

Jesus is telling us that if you can see something with your physical eyes, then don't consider it permanent. It's not permanent. It's subject to change.

I believe that it is the same for whatever has been holding you back from experiencing God's increase in your life. Whatever has seemed to be your greatest mountain, whatever appears to be your greatest barrier that is keeping you from having God's best in your life, then it is subject to change! Whatever you are going through that looks immovable and impossible in your life is subject to change!

You don't have to accept it as permanent. That is exactly what the devil wants you to do. He wants you to believe that lack in your life is permanent. Why? Because if he can get you to believe that, then your situation will never change. He wants you to believe that lie instead of the Word. He doesn't want you to believe that ... *for the things which are seen are temporal...* . Because if you begin believing this and acting on it, then defeat will become a thing of the past.

TAKE THE LIMITS OFF

Many, or maybe I should say most, Christians have put limitations on themselves as to what they can or cannot have, what they can or cannot do, and what they can or cannot be. That means they are actually self-defeating. Most Christians have become their own worst enemy. They don't even need the devil.

"What are you talking about Jerry? I don't do that?"

Yes you do if you keep saying, "Well, I just can't imagine that kind of increase coming into my life."

Your words are holding you captive (Proverbs 6:2).

So take the limits off of your life. Quit being your own worst enemy. Tell the devil if it's a fight he wants then it's a fight he's going to get. And you start by lining your words up with God's words. Say what God says and not what the devil says.

YOUR CALL TO ACTION

I want this book to be your call to action. You don't have to sit back and allow the devil to convince you that your life is not going to get any better. Don't listen to that lie. That's all it is. Don't let him persuade you into becoming passive. Don't let him cause you to believe that your life will always be like it is right now. It won't. It's going to get better. So don't allow him to form that thought and turn it into a stronghold in your mind. Just cast it down.

It doesn't matter what has happened up until now. Increase is possible. Increase is God's plan, and it is possible for you to experience it. And it's time for it to become a reality in your life.

HOW TO MAKE YOUR LIFE BETTER

Now, I know that we have discussed issues of your heart and God's ways to position yourself for experiencing increase God's way, but now I want to end this book by giving you four keys to making your life better.

#1. DREAM IT

Before you can experience increase in your life, you must dream it. Martin Luther King Jr, said in his famous speech, "I have a dream." So let me ask you today: Do you have a dream for your life?

Every person who has achieved a better life all started off by dreaming it. We talked earlier about how God's Word is designed to create an image on the inside of you of the way that He wants you to live. Experiencing increase in your life was first His dream. Now it must become your dream. And the more time you spend in His Word, the more perfected that image will become on the inside of you. God's dream for your life will become alive on the inside of you. It will cause you to wake up with an excitement that you are one day closer to His dream (and yours) becoming a reality in your life. And the more excited you become about your dream, then the more passionate you will become about it. The more passionate you become, the more determined you become. And the more determined you become, the less you think about quitting and giving up on it.

GET OVER THE PAST

One of the things that was really strong in the apostle Paul's heart was that Christians would be able to comprehend what God had in store for them.

May be able to comprehend… Ephesians 3:18

To *comprehend* means *to grasp, to conceive.* It means that you would be able to conceive the dream that God has for your life. A lot of people can't comprehend that God wants them living an exciting, wonderful life because they keep hanging on to their past experiences.

"I can't imagine ever being out of debt?"

Well, why not? Why can't you imagine being out of debt and out of financial bondage? Because you are letting past experiences keep you from it.

"Oh, but you don't understand, Jerry. I came from a long

line of people who were in debt. My grandfather was in debt. My daddy was in debt. I am in debt. Everybody I know is in debt. I can't imagine not being in debt."

Then you are the one who has got to break the mold. It doesn't have to be that way for you just because it's that way for everybody else. But you have to be able to comprehend, to grasp, or conceive being out of debt first. Do you understand what I am saying?

When you begin to believe God's Word over everything else, then it will change your image of yourself. And once that changes, then it's only a matter of time before it starts changing in the physical world. But it all starts with a dream. First God's dream, then making it your dream.

WHAT'S THE DREAM?

Thou crownest the year with thy goodness; and thy paths drop fatness.

Psalm 65:11

The word *fatness* in this scripture represents abundance.

God's dream is that you experience His goodness and His abundance as never before. Where did I get that? From the Bible. Doesn't that sound like a good dream for your life?

#2. PURSUE IT

Now to make God's dream become a reality in your life, it's going to take more than just dreaming it. It starts with dreaming it but it doesn't end there. That is just the beginning. Next, you must pursue the dream.

How do you do that?

Well, Jesus said if you believe those things which you say shall come to pass, then they will (Mark 11:23). And there's nobody that you believe more than yourself. So you must begin to say it. You must begin to declare God's dream in your life. When you hear yourself declaring God's dream for your life, then it becomes real to you.

So I would encourage you to begin to declare God's dream for your life every day. This is one way that you pursue it. Get up in the morning and declare that you are going to experience the goodness and the abundance of God like never before. Declare that increase like never before is coming into your life.

Write it down. Put it where you can see it every day. The more you begin to declare your dream, the more convinced you will become that you will experience it.

#3. STICK WITH IT

Now, no matter what happens, stick with pursuing your

dream of increase. No matter what comes your way, don't give up. Don't give in to pressure. Don't quit! Don't allow negative circumstances to cause you to give up on your dream. People who are determined to stick with it, will eventually live it. But you can never live your dream if you quit or if you give up on it.

#4. LIVE IT

If you will dream God's dream for your life, if you will pursue it, and stick with it, then eventually you will live it. In other words, it has become reality. It may not happen in one day or in one month, but give God and His Word time to work. He will come through. After all, it's His dream for your life. And He wants it to come to pass. So dream it, pursue it, stick with it, and live it!

IT'S UP TO YOU

You can change the course of your life if you really want to. But you can't do it with a negative attitude. You can't do it as long as you continue with the same old negative thought patterns. Whatever is playing on your mind right now, whatever is telling you that your life is not going to get better, whatever is telling you that increase is never coming into your life, then deal with it! Cast down those thoughts. They are not God's thoughts. Don't let the devil convince you that he is right. He's not. He's a liar!

So what's it going to be? Are you going to experience

increase God's way? I believe you are. But it has everything to do with your decision. I can't make the decision for you, all I can do is show you in the Word what God says, but it's up to you if it ever comes to pass.

I want to leave you with this: God wants to crown your life with His goodness. He wants you to experience abundance like you have never experienced it before. God wants to increase you more and more. He wants the past barriers that have held you back to come crashing down. Now, can you dream this?

This is His dream for you. If you can dream it and you are willing to pursue it and you're willing to stick with it, then there's coming a time when you will look around and realize that you are living it!

About the Author

Dr. Jerry Savelle, known world-wide as a founding father in the Word of faith and a leader in the Body of Christ, motivates and teaches people that they are destined to win in every area of life.

Since 1969, Dr. Savelle has ministered in more than 3,000 churches and 26 nations. He has overseas offices in United Kingdom, Australia, Canada, Tanzania, with his USA headquarters in Crowley, Texas.

He has authored more than 40 books, including his bestseller, *If Satan Can't Steal Your Joy, He Can't Keep Your Goods.* Through his books, TV broadcast, *Adventures in Faith* magazine, and other ministry resources, Dr. Savelle is teaching millions to live a life of faith and victory.

Since 1978, Dr. Savelle has actively ministered in Africa, establishing churches, bible schools and meeting physical needs through humanitarian efforts. In 1996 he launched *Chariots of Light Christian Motorcycle Club* as an evangelistic outreach of JSMI that ministers to those outside the church walls. In order to disciple believers, no matter where they live, he has designed a Bible Correspondence School to train up the next generation of believers.

Dr. Savelle and his wife, Carolyn, are also founding Pastors of Heritage of Faith Christian Center in Crowley, Texas. They are the proud parents of two daughters, Jerriann Savelle Bridges and Terri Savelle Foy who reside with their husbands and (combined) six children in Crowley, Texas.

To order related material,
call, write, or visit our website
for further information.

Jerry Savelle Ministries International
P.O. Box 748
Crowley, TX 76036
817/297-3155
www.jerrysavelle.org

Other books by Jerry Savelle

Receive God's Best

Free to be Yourself

The God of the Breakthrough Will Visit Your House

If Satan Can't Steal Your Dreams, He Can't
Control Your Destiny

Free at Last from Oppression

Free at Last from Old Habits

Thoughts – The Battle between Your Ears

Expect the Extraordinary

In the Footsteps of a Prophet

The Last Frontier

Take Charge of Your Financial Destiny

From Devastation to Restoration

Walking in Divine Favor

Turning Your Adversity into Victory

Honoring Your Heritage of Faith

Don't Let Go of Your Dreams

Faith Building Daily Devotionals

The Force of Joy

If Satan Can't Steal Your Joy, He Can't
Keep Your Goods

A Right Mental Attitude

The Nature of Faith

Sharing Jesus Effectively

How to Overcome Financial Famine

You're Somebody Special to God

For those who don't know Jesus, would you like to know Him?

If you were to die today, where would you spend eternity? If you have accepted Jesus Christ as your personal Lord and Savior, you can be assured that when you die, you will go directly into the presence of God in Heaven. If you have not accepted Jesus as your personal Lord and Savior, is there any reason why you can't make Jesus the Lord of your life right now? Please pray this prayer out loud, and as you do, pray with a sincere and trusting heart, and you will be born again.

Dear God in Heaven,

I come to You in the Name of Jesus to receive salvation and eternal life. I believe that Jesus is Your Son. I believe that He died on the cross for my sins, and that You raised Him from the dead. I receive Jesus now into my heart and make Him the Lord of my life. Jesus, come into my heart. I welcome You as my Lord and Savior. Father, I believe Your Word that says I am now saved. I confess with my mouth that I am saved and born again. I am now a child of God.